MY BIG FAT FONT BOOK

JAMES HARLESS

CONTENTS

House Music

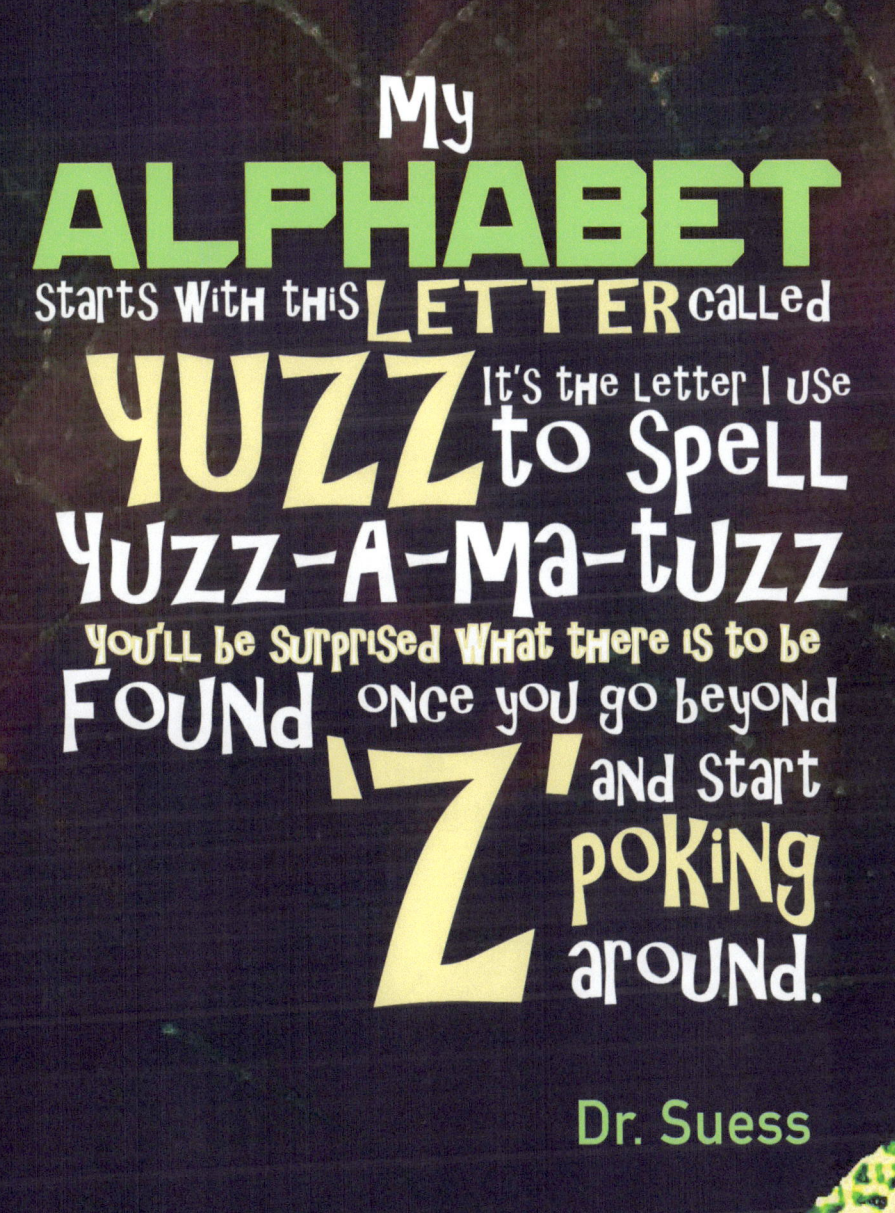

My
ALPHABET
starts with this LETTER called
YUZZ It's the letter I use
to spell
Yuzz-a-ma-tuzz
You'll be surprised what there is to be
FOUND once you go beyond
'Z' and start
poking
around.

Dr. Suess

be
happy
for this
this **moment**
moment
is your
Life

Omar Khayyam

Tower Print

FROM
CARING
COMES
COURAGE
Lao Tzu

Hermeneus One

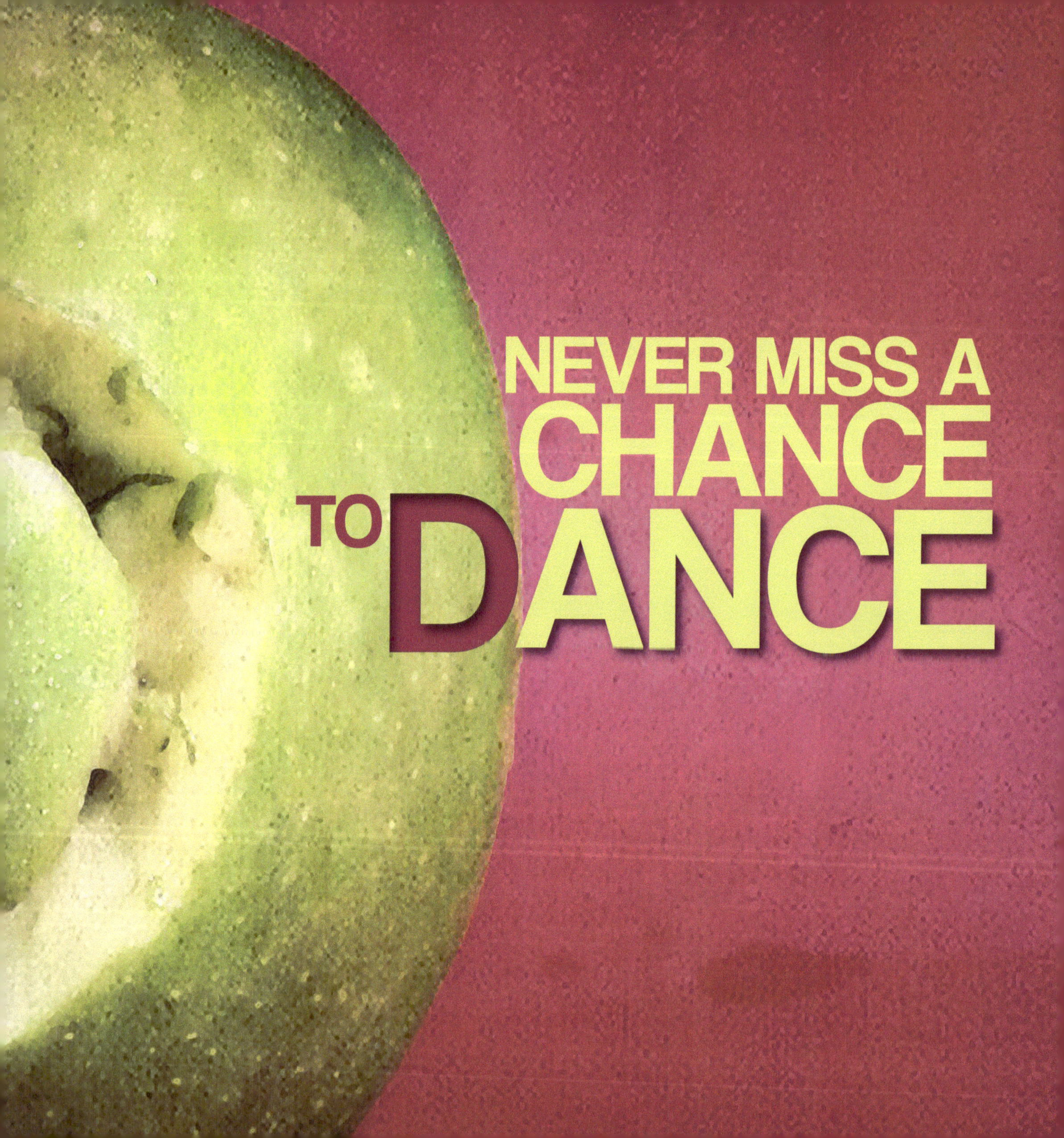
NEVER MISS A
CHANCE
TO DANCE

Coolvetica

we did not realize
we were making
memories
we just knew
we were having
fun

Perfect Dos

POLKADOT
CRAZY

PLAY EVERY

GAME

AS IF IT IS YOUR LAST ONE

GUY LAFLEUR

DESIGN

BARON NEUE

BE **HAPPY** AND *smile*

my *life* is so much more

INTERESTING

inside my head

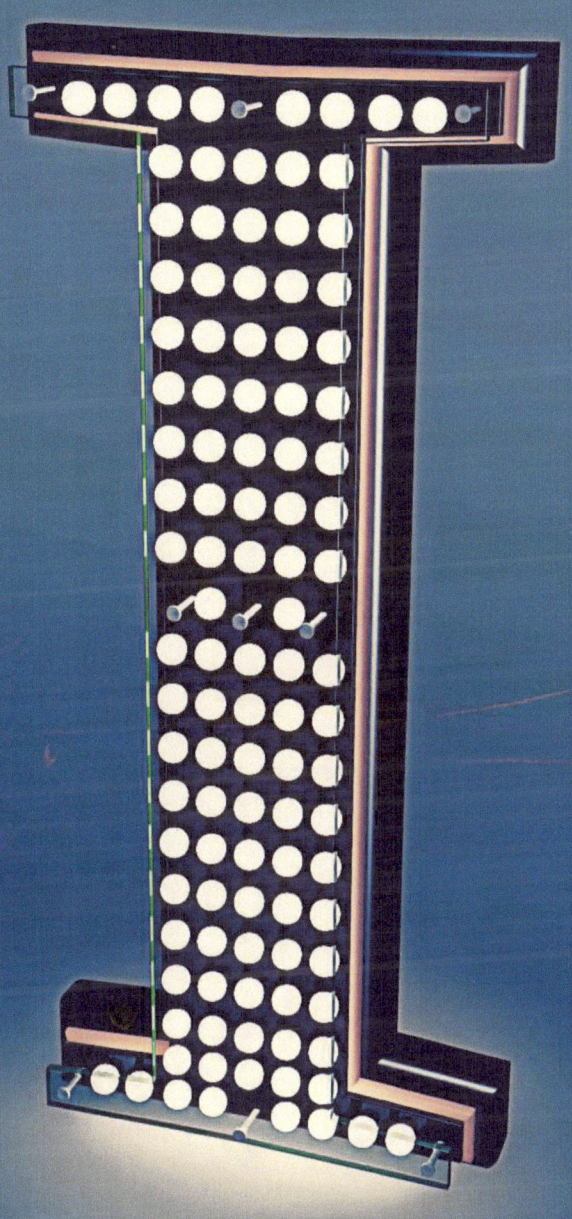

Vinegar

FINE STYLE

Northern Lights Script

Keep true to the Dreams of thy youth

Friedrich von Schiller

Love is patientkind

1 Corinthians 13

Radagund

noun.

MIND

**a beautiful servant
a dangerous master**

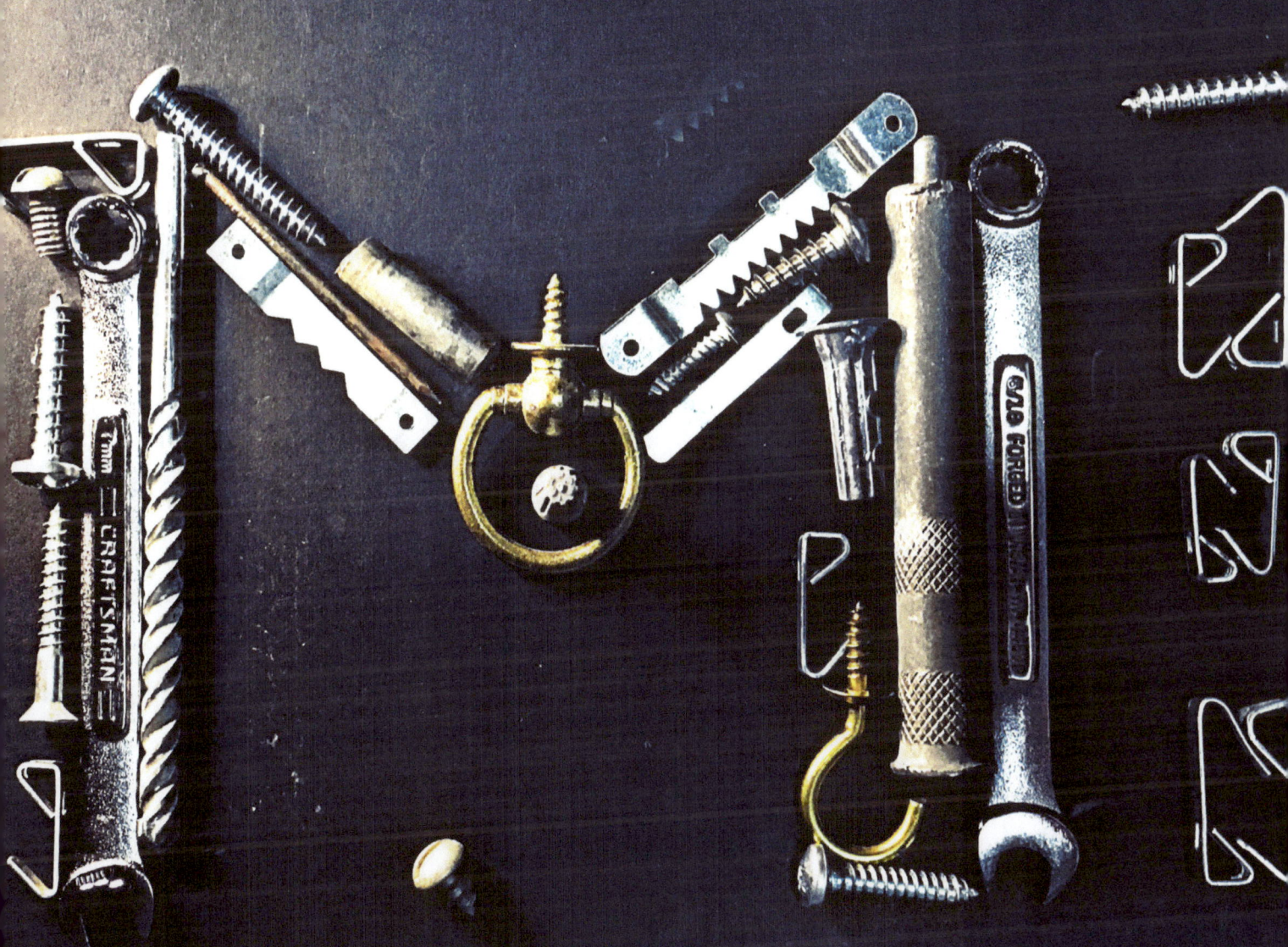

VIDEOPAC

NEOTERIC

IF YOU NEVER GIVE YOU WILL BE UP SUCCESSFUL

DAN O'BRIEN

WHEN YOU
OBSERVE
RATHER THAN REACT
YOU RECLAIM
YOUR
POWER

DENISE LINN

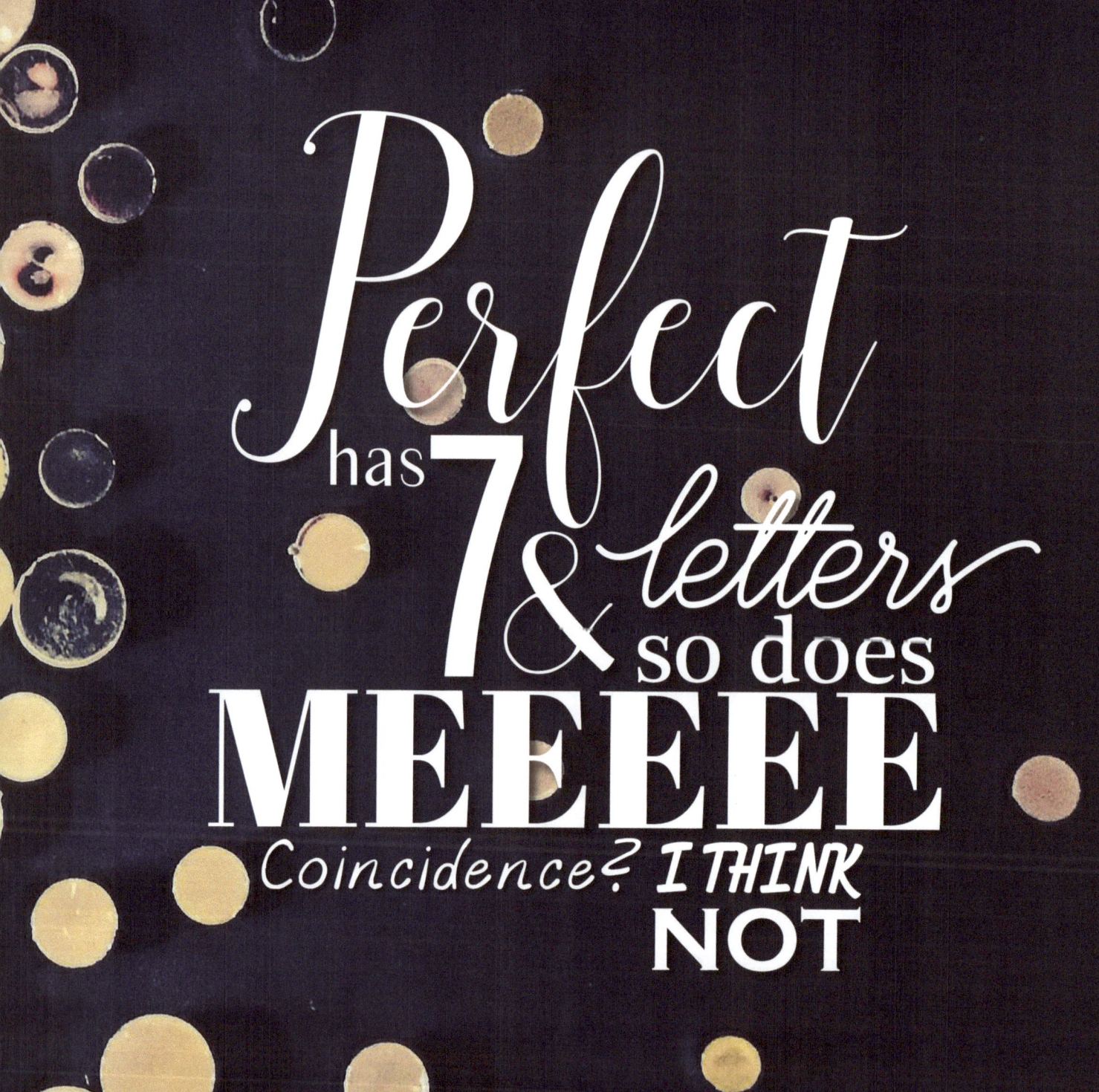

Ahattom

Syouwa Retro
Pop

it is always too early to

QUIT

RAISE YOUR thoughts NOT YOUR fists

Matshona Shliwayo

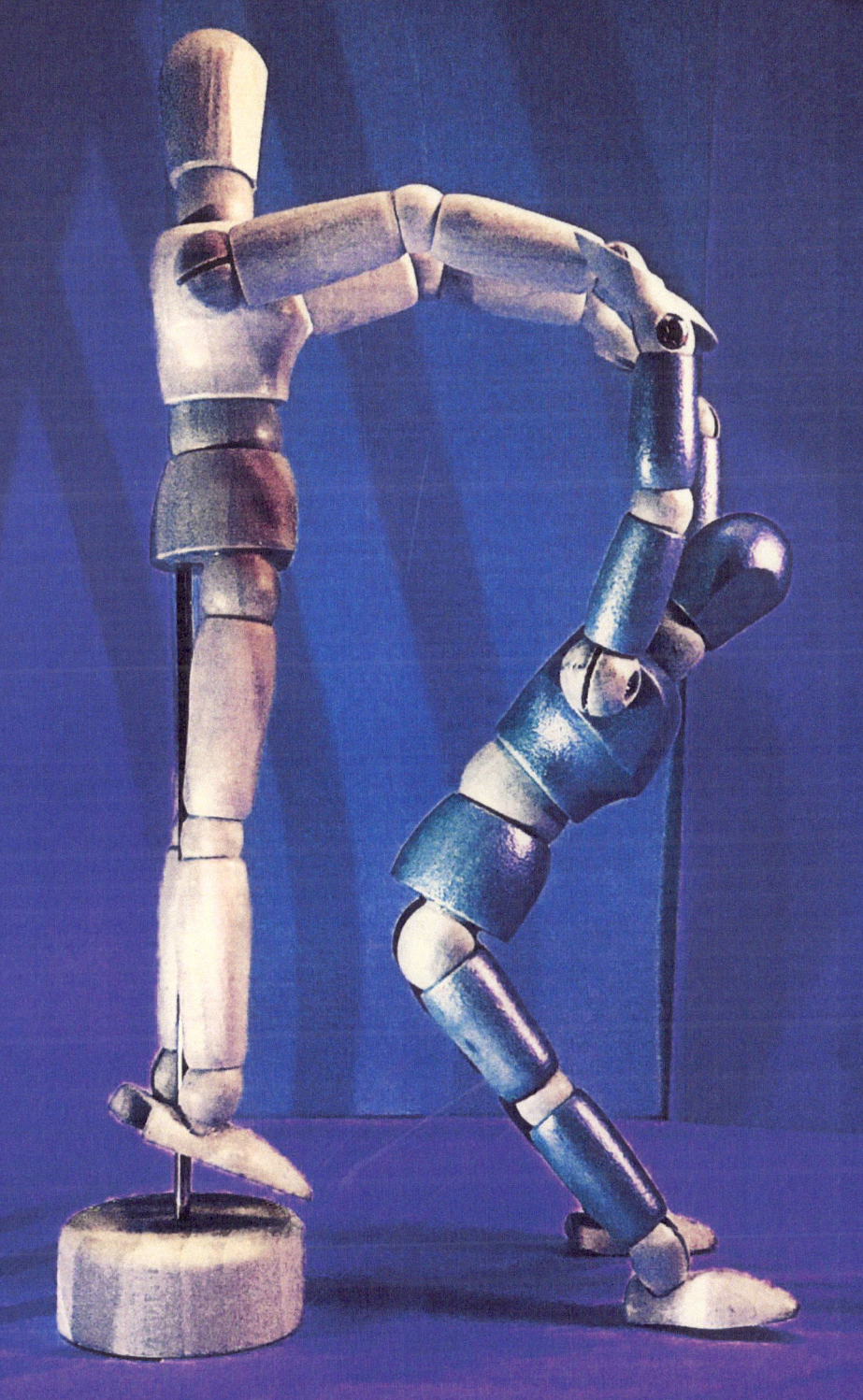

delouisville

CHUCK NOON

Jeanne Mance

the only way to go is

UP

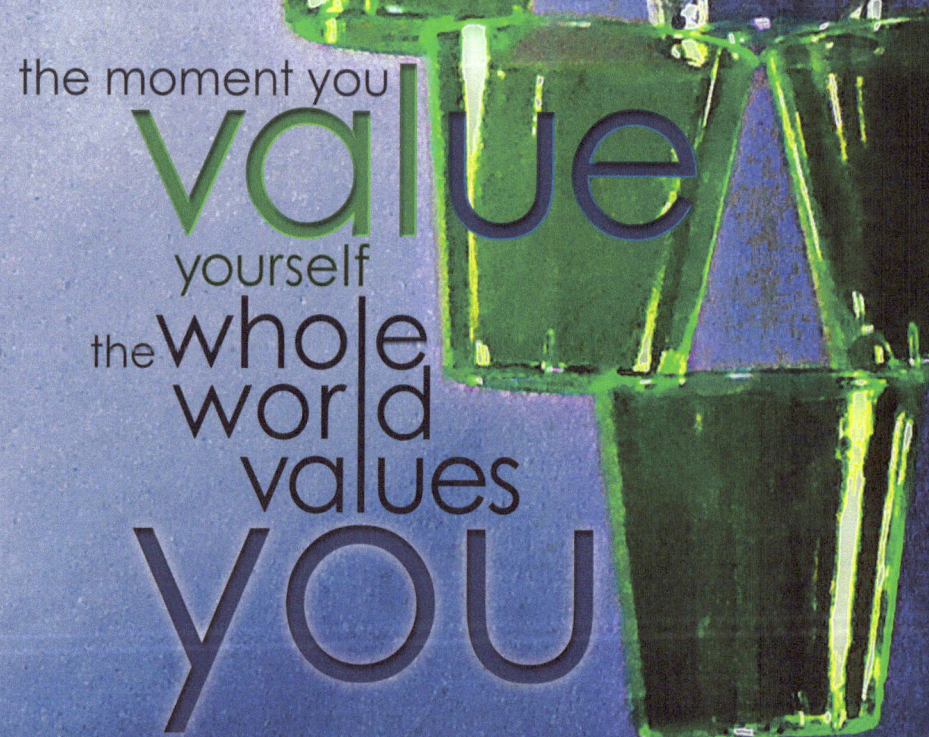

the moment you
value
yourself
the whole
world
values
you

Harbhajan Singh Yogi

Century Gothic

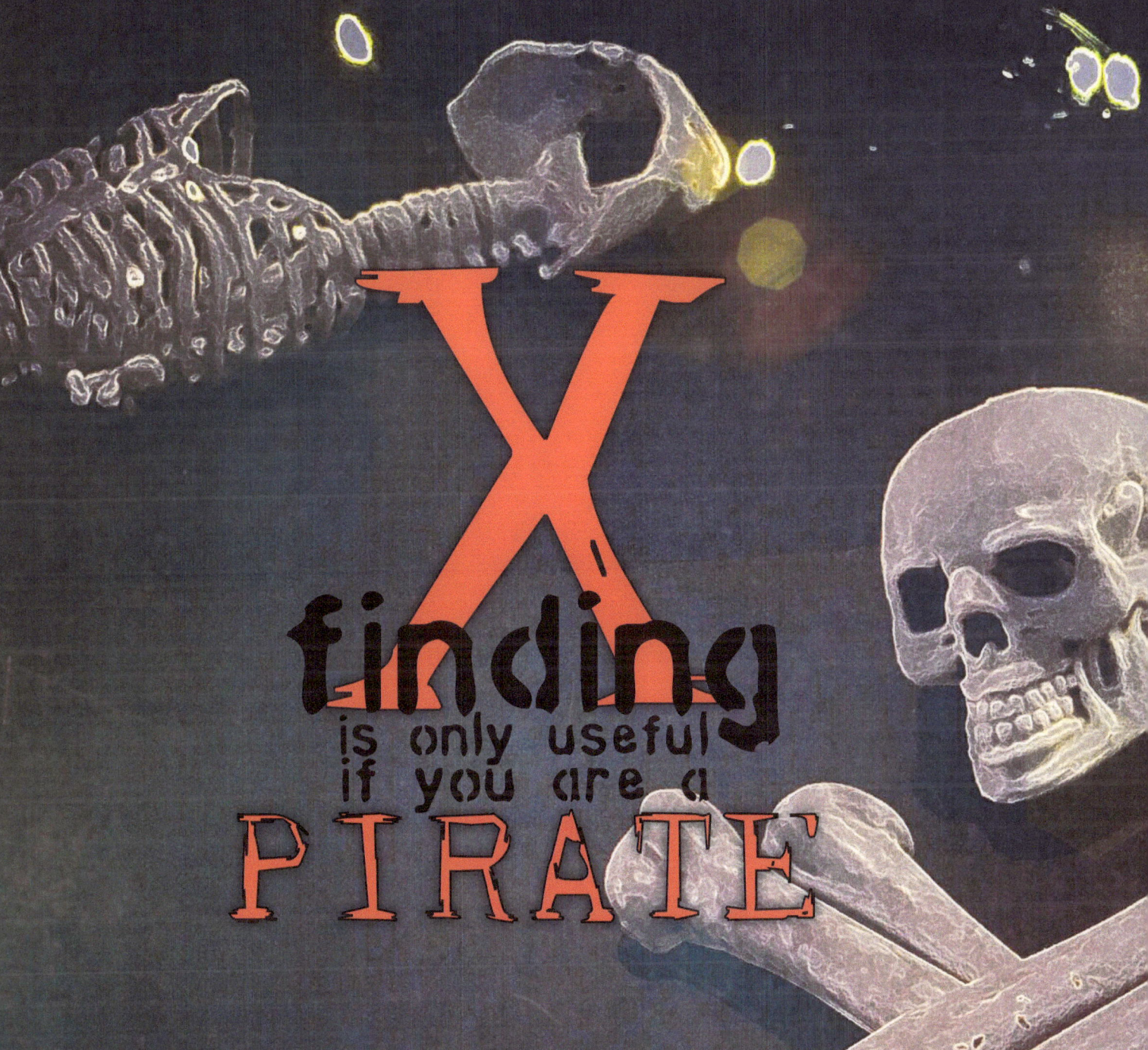

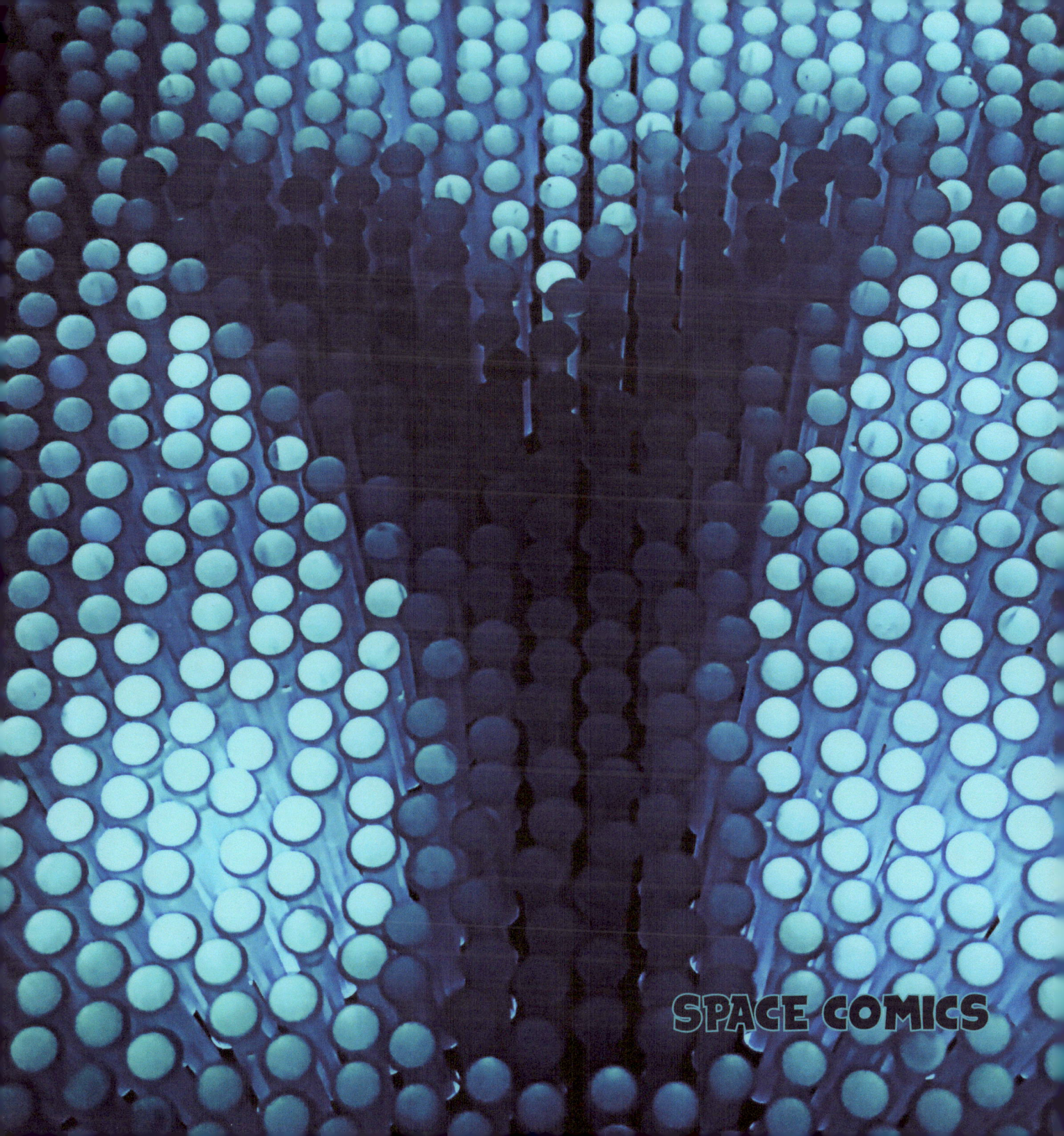

acephimere

BACK TO
zero

Queen of Heaven

LCD PHONE

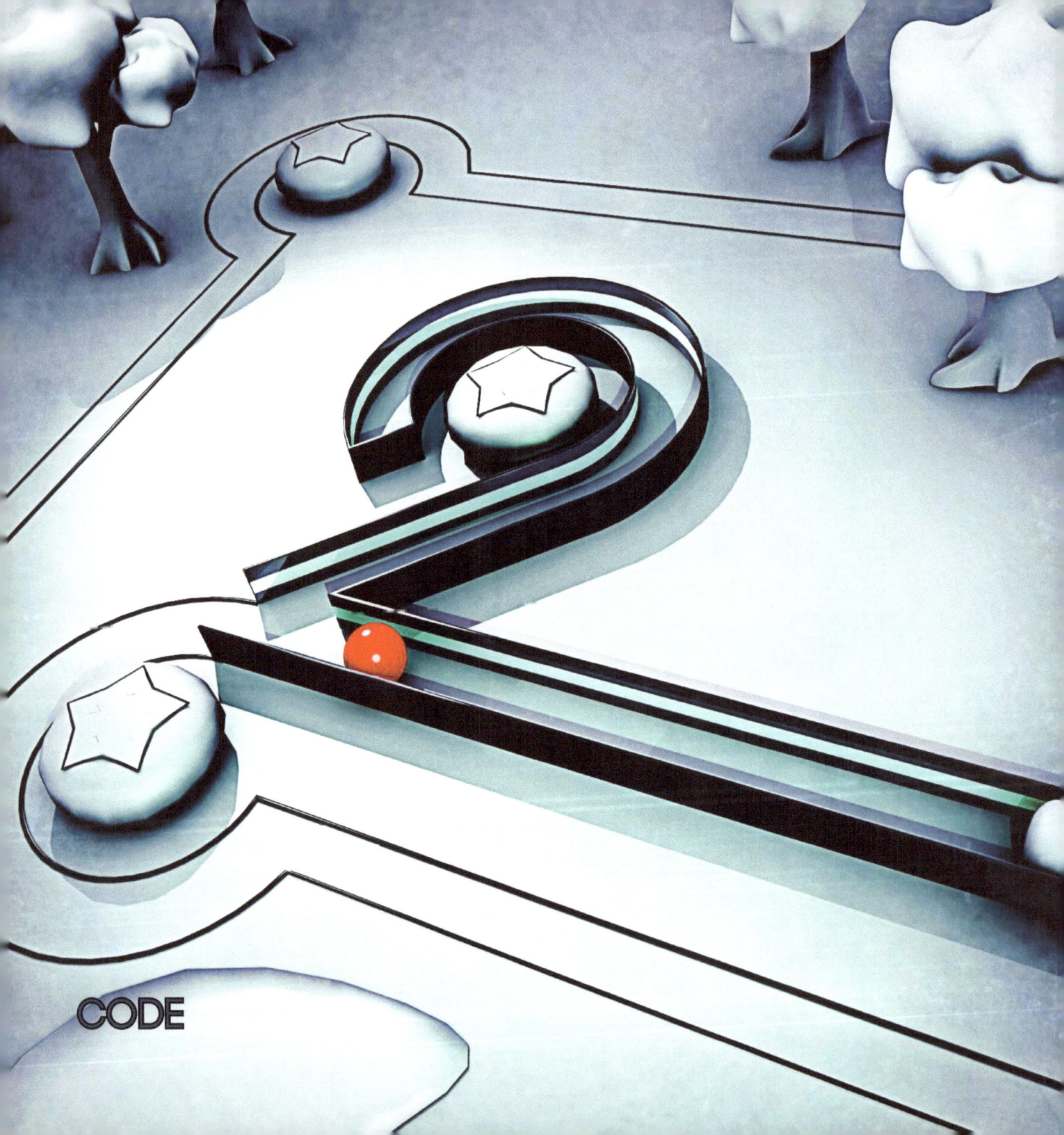

QUICKSAND

ALIEN ENCOUNTER

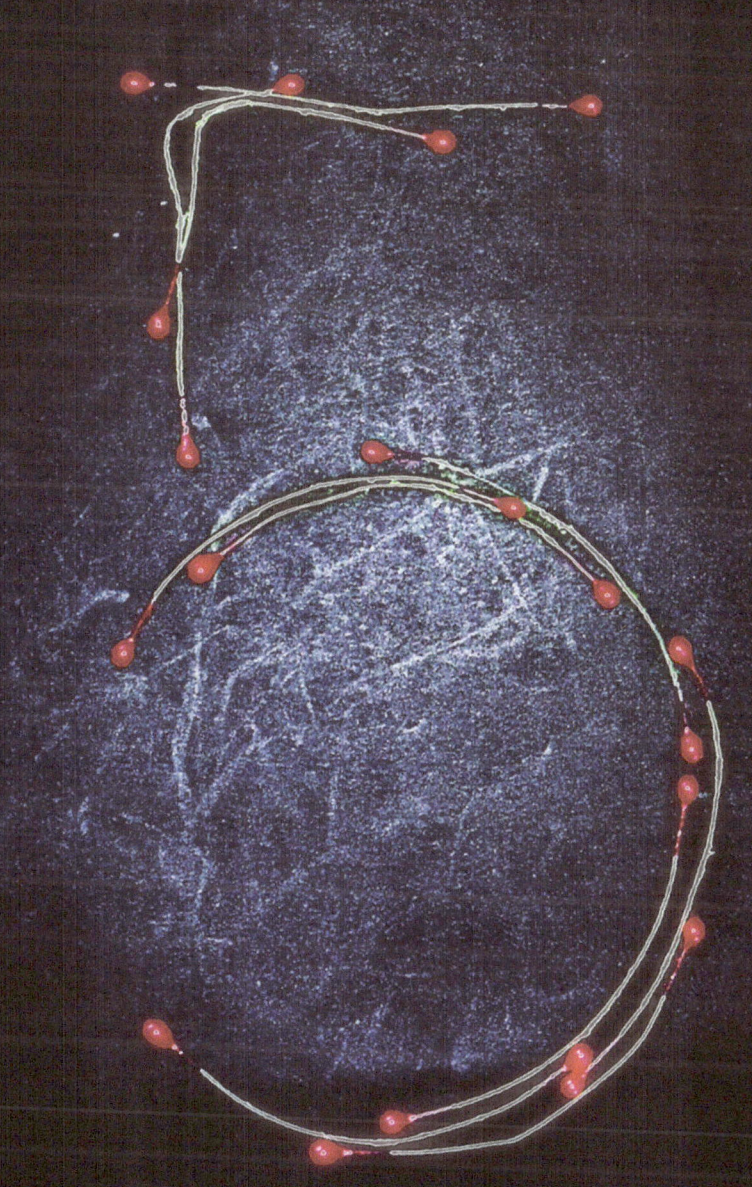

Champagne & Limousine

DOLCE VITA

Renzo

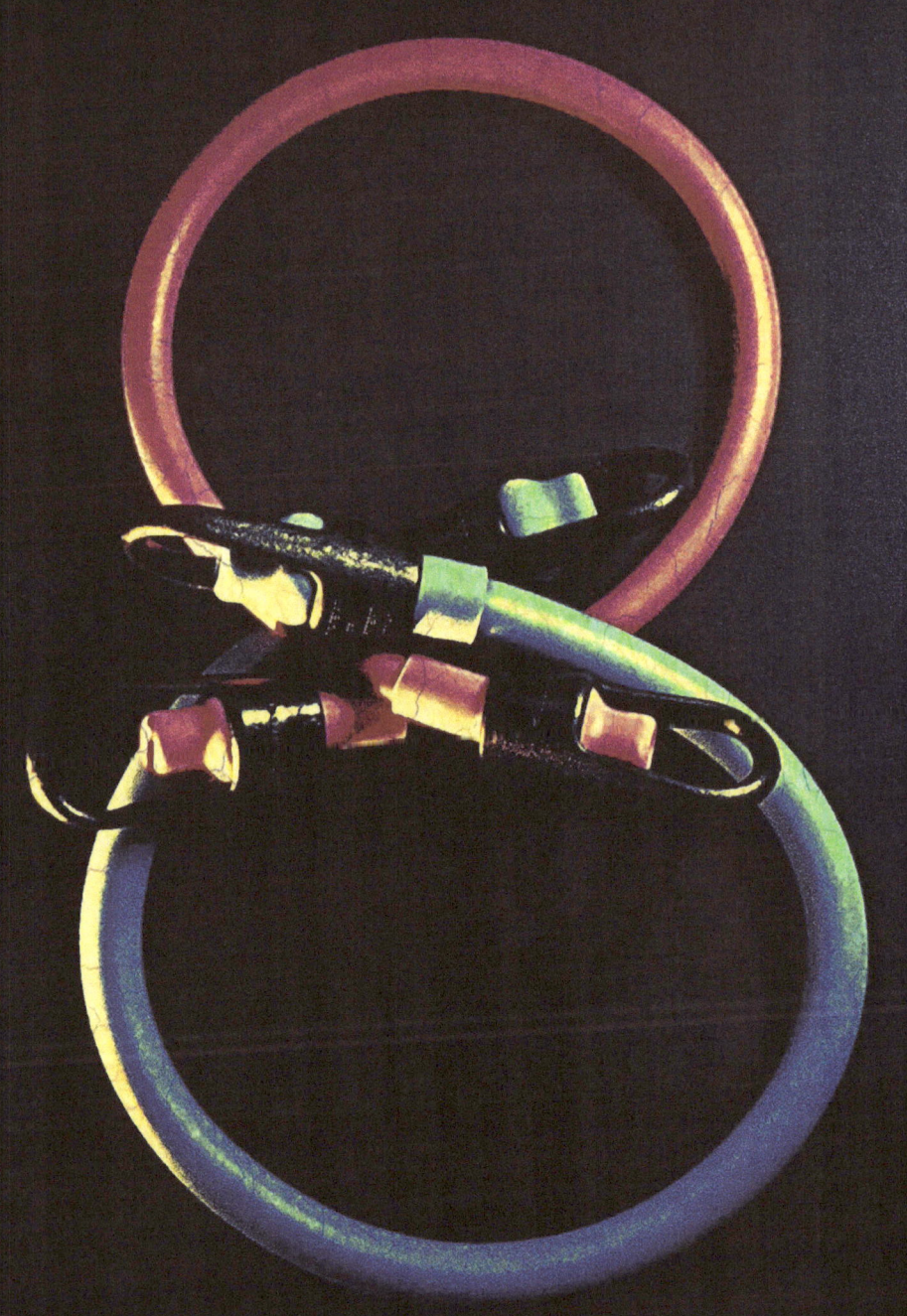

Lumnia

Keep Calm

ABOUT THE AUTHOR

James Harless lives in Connecticut where he currently attends Central Connecticut State University as a Graphic Design student. Originally from Georgia, James began making his mark in the graphic arts while attending Gordon State College. Some of his notable credits include the 2013 Enmark Savannah River Bridge Run T-Shirt design competition, and the current logo and t-shirt design for Savannah Pride, Inc.

If you would like to see more work by James Harless, please follow him on social media:

www.facebook.com/JamesTHarless
www.instagram.com/jtharless